Color Your Kingdom

Color Your Kingdom

Illustrations © 2017 Ashley Villers

www.ashleyvillers.com
Instagram: @winterTHIRTEEN
Twitter: @winterTHIRTEEN

ISBN: 978-0-692-95559-8

This project started as a single page and tool to teach drawing and colored pencil techniques while live streaming on Twitch Creative. Fourteen months and over twenty drawings later, I have decided to share the project with more than just my Twitch community.

These works of art were all hand-drawn with pen and ink. They depict some of my favorite animals and plants, with combinations symbolic of strength, beauty, honor, and courage.

I am so happy to share my art with you and excited to see how you interpret these pieces and give the work life.

I recommend using colored pencils for this book as the weight of the paper may not take wet materials such as ink or paint. For best results, place a piece or two of scrap paper under the page that you're coloring to prevent materials from bleeding through onto the next page of art.

A huge thank you to my community for all of the support, encouragement, and help throughout this project.

Happy coloring!

Made in the USA
San Bernardino, CA
03 December 2017